What Is Water?

by Robin Nelson

first step nonfiction

Lerner Publications Company · Minneapolis

Water is all around us.

Most of the earth is covered by water.

Water can be a **liquid.**

Rain is water.

Water can be a **gas.**

Steam is water.

Water can be a **solid.**

Ice is water.

Water can be cold.

Water can be hot.

Water is wet.

Water can be heavy.

Water is **clear.**

Water has no taste.

Plants and animals need
water to live.

We need water to live.

18

Rainbows

Did you know that a rainbow is made with water? We see a rainbow when sunlight shines into rain. To see a rainbow you must be facing a rain shower. The sun must be shining behind you. The sunlight hits the raindrops and bounces back to you. This creates all of the colors of a rainbow. You can create your own rainbow using a garden hose. Stand with the sun behind you and spray the hose in front of you.

Water Facts

Water is made of very small particles. Each particle is so small that you can't even see it with a microscope.

Water is the only thing that can come in three forms—solid, liquid, and gas.

Water covers three-fourths of the earth. Only a very small amount is freshwater that we can use and drink.

A person could live for only about one week without water.

We live on the "Water Planet." If you look at the earth from space, it looks like a blue and white ball. The blue is liquid water. The white is water as a gas called water vapor.

People in the United States drink more than 1 billion glasses of tap water each day.

The human body is about 75% water. An elephant is 70% water. A pineapple is 80% water. A tomato is 95% water.

Glossary

 clear – easy to see through

 gas – something that is light and fills up space

 liquid – something you can pour

 solid – something with a shape; not a liquid or a gas

 steam – water that has become a gas from heat; steam looks like thin smoke

Index

The photographs in this book are reproduced through the courtesy of: Corbis Royalty Free Images, front cover; © Diane Meyer, pp. 2 (top left), 8, 22 (second from bottom); © Todd Strand/ Independent Picture Service, p. 2 (top right); National Science Foundation, p. 2 (bottom left); © Joerg Boetel/Photo Agora, p. 2 (bottom right); NASA, p. 3; © Trinity Muller/Independent Picture Service, pp. 4, 22 (middle); © Ken Layman/Photo Agora, p. 5; PhotoDisc, pp. 6, 13, 16, 22 (second from top); © David Kreider/Photo Agora, pp. 7, 22 (bottom); © Stephen Graham Photography, p. 9; © Jeff Greenberg/Photo Agora, p. 10; © Colleen Sexton/Independent Picture Service, p. 11; Stockbyte, p. 12; © Jerome Rogers/Independent Picture Service, pp. 14, 22 (top); © Robert Maust/Photo Agora, pp. 15, 17.

The illustration on page 18 is by Tim Seeley.

Lerner Publications Company
A division of Lerner Publishing Group
241 First Avenue North
Minneapolis, MN 55401 U.S.A.

Website address: www.lernerbooks.com

Library of Congress Cataloging-in-Publication Data

Nelson, Robin, 1971–
  What is water? / by Robin Nelson.
    p. cm. — (First step nonfiction)
  Summary: An introduction to water and its properties.
  ISBN-13: 978–0–8225–4588–0 (lib. bdg. : alk. paper)
  ISBN-10: 0–8225–4588–8 (lib. bdg. : alk. paper)
  1. Water—Juvenile literature. 2. Hydrology—Juvenile literature. [1. Water.] I. Title.
II. Series.
  GB662.3 .N46 2003
  546'.22—dc21   2002007192

Manufactured in the United States of America
2 3 4 5 6 7 – DP – 10 09 08 07 06 05